Introduction

This guide is for adults caring for children wh
It has been written to accompany a children's book called **Someone has died suddenly**. You need a copy of this book at hand before you read this guide.
If you do not have this book call **01484 559909.**

This guide takes you through the content of the children's book and the academic thinking behind it. Page 11 gives information on what else you can do to help suddenly bereaved children. Page 12 gives specific guidance for teachers.

In addition to reading this short guide, there are guidance notes at the front of **Someone has died suddenly**. There are also lists of support agencies at the back of that book.

About the Amy and Tom project

The book and this guide are by the Amy & Tom project, which supports suddenly bereaved families. The Amy & Tom project is run by Brake, the road safety charity.

The book and this guide have been developed in consultation with experts in sudden child bereavement and bereaved parents and children, and piloted with bereaved families to ensure they offer the best possible support.

Thank you for taking the time to use the book and help children. If you wish to make a donation to Brake, go to www.brake.org.uk.

The reality of sudden deaths

Every day in the UK, hundreds of people die suddenly, devastating families. These deaths include disasters such as road crashes, suicide, murder, heart attacks and other sudden fatal illnesses.

Many of the bereaved relatives are children, who are suffering the death of a parent or guardian, or both parents or guardians, or a sibling or siblings, when it was least expected, usually in the prime of life, and often in very violent circumstances.

Sometimes, a surviving child witnessed family members dying, either at the scene or in hospital. A child may also have been involved in a disaster that killed their loved ones and may themselves have serious injuries that will last a lifetime, such as brain injury or spinal injury, or have a surviving parent or sibling who has serious injuries.

Sometimes, for example in a road crash, a child's entire family is killed and they are the sole survivor, meaning they are grieving and also facing the very difficult challenge of adjusting to a new life in a new home with new adult carers.

A suddenly bereaved child always needs love, support and care to enable them to grieve and have the best chance of a full and happy life. **You can help**.

How do children grieve?

Children are often described as 'the forgotten mourners' because they are frequently excluded from having a full and active role in the grieving process. This exclusion is usually, and misguidedly, in the belief that the less a child knows, and the more they are diverted from the topic of the death or deaths, the less it will hurt them.

In reality, children have a right to know what has happened, and a right to grieve, just like everyone else. Hiding a child from the truth is only storing up trouble and potential resentment for the future. There is a wealth of academic research to show that it is much better to tell children things than to keep them in the dark. Children have active imaginations and if you don't tell them things, their imaginations will fill in the gaps with something that may be even more horrendous than the truth.[1]

Children grieve in different ways at different times. At different times they may cry, get angry, be quiet, be noisy, talk about the person who died, not talk about them, or play or behave as though nothing had happened.

All these reactions and many more are natural. Your job is to help support children through their grief, answering their questions honestly, and helping them feel safe and loved.

Introducing Amy and Tom

The book is narrated by two children – Amy and Tom – who have both been bereaved suddenly and are recovering from their grief. Many children do not know anyone else who has been bereaved, and this can make them feel isolated. The characters Tom and Amy can help them feel they are not alone. Through simple actions Tom and Amy illustrate and describe a range of emotions from anger and sadness, to feeling better.

Often, Tom and Amy are pictured doing ordinary, every-day things, such as eating cornflakes, walking to school, and even bouncing on space hoppers. These are things that a child can relate to, and which show that bereaved children can have fun too.

The children's book is for all children, whatever their age.

The book works on different levels for children of different ages – older children can read the text and younger children can look at the colourful images and listen to the descriptions read by the parent or carer.

It is very important that the book appeals to children of different ages. This is because there is often more than one bereaved child in a family unit. It is very appropriate to read the book with a group of siblings.

Grieving children should not be talked down to, or kept in the dark.

They should be given the opportunity to ask questions and share their feelings.

The book encourages discussion and honesty between children and adult carers, using simple language and an open tone. The book includes:

- Opportunities for adult carers to share information about what has happened
- Questions for the children, to encourage them to share their feelings and thoughts
- Opportunities for children to write down memories and carry out activities
- A promise for adult carers and children to read and sign, to enable them to support each other through their grief

These are simple ways to help children in distress to share emotions and gain support.

Your well-being is important too.

If you are a parent and have suffered the same bereavement, you should give your own emotional needs as much priority as a child's emotional needs. You will be better able to support your child or children and give them a happy home environment if you are recovering from your own trauma. Go to page 40 of the book to find out how to access support for yourself through the NHS, privately or through a charity. Depending on the details of your bereavement, there may be other help available to you locally that is not listed on this page - ask your GP or call a general support charity such as The Samaritans (08457 909090) or Cruse Bereavement Care (0844 4779400) for help and more contacts.

If you are a professional then you may find yourself emotionally affected by the bereavement of a child or children in your care. It is helpful for you to have a regular confidential conversation with someone who can provide you with a listening ear and professional support. This could be an experienced colleague or an independent professional such as a therapist, depending on your working environment. Hopefully, your employment policy includes this kind of support. If not, ask for the policy to be rewritten so this support is included.

A step by step guide to the contents of the children's book

The book starts with an introduction to death, shock and sadness. It then gives opportunities for frank discussion about what happened, what it feels like to die and what happens to the body. This is followed by different emotions that bereaved children often feel and how to cope. The book ends with a section on how to remember the person who has died, including space to write down memories in the book itself.

It is difficult for children to comprehend the enormity of death, and to understand why it has happened. **Why did they die?** (page 3) covers the kind of questions children may ask right away. Younger children may not grasp the finality of death and think, unless told, that the dead person will wake up.[2]

I don't believe it has happened! (page 4) Children, like adults, find it hard to understand that something terrible has changed their lives forever, and will often be in complete denial about what has happened. The initial shock of the death is often replayed in the child's mind, for example on waking up each morning.[3]

Children may feel unwell, or be visibly very upset. Some children, particularly younger children, may not appear to react to the death at all, or may say things that seem insensitive, such as asking to go out to play straight after being told. **All about shock** (page 5) explains the emotional and physical reactions to shock and looks at comforts such as food, warmth and love. These things can help children feel better.[4]

Like adults, children dip in and out of grief, but feelings of sadness can seem overwhelming and never-ending. **Feeling sad** (page 6) shows children that their unhappiness is a normal part of the grieving process. It also reassures them that they won't feel sad forever, and that good things will happen again.[5]

Strong feelings (page 7) explains that children may have powerful, new and frightening feelings. This is a useful page for helping childen understand that all these feelings are normal and that life will get better.

Why? is the most common question asked by a child. **What happened?** (page 8) helps children ask questions and get them answered by you. It is better for children to know the facts than to be kept in the dark, however horrific the circumstances, because they may imagine something even worse.[6]

It can be reassuring for children to know that everything possible was done to save the life of their special person. **All about the emergency services** and **All about the police** (pages 9 and 10) describes the kind of care and treatment that is given by paramedics, police, firefighters and doctors. Many emergency workers are happy to talk to bereaved families.[7] You may feel it is appropriate to find out if an emergency service is able to talk with a child and you about what happened.

Children, particularly boys, are often fascinated by the details of a death, and may want to know exactly what happened, even if this seems gory to adults. Boys are more likely to ask about the details – girls usually want to know too, but may be more reluctant to ask. **Why do some people die suddenly?** (pages 11 and 12) explains why a person's body stopped working.

Very young children may not have been taught about death, and may be very interested in what death feels like, and whether the dead person felt any pain. **What does it feel like to die?** (page 13) deals with children's natural curiosity about the death and re-enforces the message that dead people don't have any feelings.[8]

The role of A&E and Intensive Care Units are discussed in **Dying in a hospital** (page 14), to help children understand how hospitals try to save lives and why this often doesn't work when someone is hurt badly or very ill. Families often spend tortuous days, weeks or even months waiting in a hospital while doctors try to save somebody's life and then ultimately fail. Being caught between hope and the likelihood of death during this time is an additional, extreme stress for families who are then ultimately bereaved.

Giving parts of a dead body to someone who is alive to help them get better (pages 15 and 16) raises the issue of transplants and how organs or tissue from a dead person can sometimes be used to help other people. For some families, it is a source of comfort to know that a dead person's body has been used to help other people live, although donation is not possible in all cases.

A step by step guide to the contents of the children's book (Continued)

Children, like adults, are often encouraged not to view a body and to remember the dead person as they were. However research suggests that it is better to give children a choice, based on clear communication of what a body will look like (some bodies are very badly damaged and do not look like the person at all). **Can I see their body?** and **Seeing a body** (pages 17 and 18) helps the adult carer or parent to explain what a body looks like and then gives them a chance to offer the child a choice to see or not to see a body. Viewing a dead body can help children to understand the finality of death and to say goodbye to their loved one.[9]

After a sudden death, there will usually be a post-mortem examination to determine the cause of death. **What happens to my special person's body now?** (page 19) discusses the role of a post-mortem examination in finding out how the person died.

Children want to know what happens to the body, and may ask questions about burning bodies, or bodies decaying underground. **What happens to the body then?** (page 20) looks at the differences between burial and cremation and what each process involves.[10]

We are having a funeral (page 21) helps children to prepare for what to expect at a funeral and to open a discussion about attending. Some adults may think that it is inappropriate for a child to attend a funeral. However, children may benefit from taking part if they know what to expect. They may also contribute good ideas about what should happen at a funeral.[11]

Common feeling 1: I want to cry (page 23) shows crying as a normal part of the grieving process. Children should be encouraged to express their own emotions, instead of copying the behaviour of a parent or carer, who may be 'putting on a brave front'.[12]

Common feeling 2: I'm really angry (page 24) gives examples of safe ways to express anger, such as hitting a cushion. Children should be encouraged to channel their anger into behaviour that does not harm themselves or other people.[13]

Common feeling 3: It was my fault (page 25) tackles common feelings of guilt children experience after a sudden death. It is vitally important to tell children they are not to blame for a death. Some children believe their thoughts or behaviour are to blame for a death.[14]

Common feeling 4: I feel alone (page 26) deals with the isolation that children often feel following a bereavement. Children can be excluded or even teased by other children because someone has died. They can also feel lonely if they do not know any other children who have lost a loved one.[15]

Common feeling 5: Things that other people say (page 27) highlights some of the insensitive sayings children hear from well-meaning friends or adults, such as 'you're the man of the house now' or 'you're young, you'll get over it'. Children may act like 'little adults' following a death, but they should not be encouraged to take on the responsibilities of the dead person.[16]

Common feeling 6: I just don't want to do anything any more (page 28) deals with feelings of despondency and lack of motivation.[17] Encouraging children to take up a new activity or hobby can help them to feel normal again.

Common feeling 7: I keep thinking about it (page 29) explores the difficult memories and thoughts children may experience, whether or not they witnessed the event. Encouraging children to write down or draw their experiences can help them to make sense of their feelings.

Common feeling 8: Are other people I know going to die suddenly? (page 30) explores the common fears that children experience following the death of someone close. Children may be excessively worried about the health or safety of surviving relatives and friends, and will need reassurance.

It can be difficult for children to think about the future, and many worry that they will always feel sad. **When will I feel better?** and **Having fun is good for you** (pages 31 and 32) reassure children that they will have fun and feel happy again.

How to remember (pages 33 and 34) deals with ways of keeping memories alive by remembering significant places or events, or creating a memory box for special mementos.[18] The idea for a memory box is inspired by the children's bereavement charity Winston's Wish.[19]

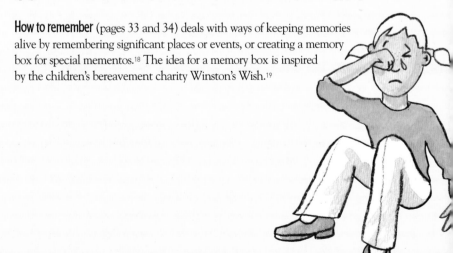

A step by step guide to the contents of the children's book (Continued)

Bereaved children can feel stressed and worried that they will forget important things about a person. **All about them** (page 35) encourages children to write down the important things they remember about their special person.[20]

Expressing grief creatively through drawing or writing can really benefit children. **My poem** (page 36) uses a simple formula to enable children to create their own poem about the person who died. You may need to encourage a child to come up with good ideas for this page by asking them open-ended questions. The result can be really worth it.

Many children find it intimidating to go back to school (or a pre-school learning environment) simply after a holiday. It's so much harder going back after a loved one has died. **Back to school** (page 37) acknowledges this challenge and gives practical advice. If you are a parent, show this guide and the accompanying book to the head teacher and discuss your child's needs. If you are a teacher, there is further advice for you on providing support on page 12.

Children often find it hard to express their emotions, so it can be helpful to set out 'rules' allowing them to express themselves, and saying how they'd like to be treated. **Our promise** (page 38) is based on postcards developed by the Childhood Bereavement Network that allow children to choose how their parents or carers interact with them.[21]

What else you can do to help

As well as helping children to read the book *Someone has died suddenly* there are other things you can do to help.

General support and signposting:

- Provide general practical and emotional support, after studying this guide and the accompanying children's book carefully to ensure your support is empathetic and appropriate. Practical support could include informing a child's nursery or school about the bereavement, and the need for the child to be given support in the nursery or school environment.

- Help children access therapy and additional support resources such as bereavement websites (see page 40 of the children's book).

Child protection:

If you are a professional helping a bereaved family, watch out for warning signs of parents who are struggling to cope and inform social services if you are concerned for a child's safety. Due to alcohol or drug abuse, or mental illness, some vulnerable bereaved families may be, at least temporarily, unable to care for children without support from social services, other family members, or good health care. With this support, it can be possible to prevent a complete breakdown of a family.

Specific advice for teachers

Telling other pupils

Talk to the child and their parent or carer about what they want. Some children find it helpful for a teacher to tell their class about the bereavement, but other children may want to tell only a group of friends themselves.

Allow time out

Let bereaved children take short breaks from class or assembly when they are upset. Give them somewhere safe and quiet they can go where there is caring adult supervision, no questions asked – such as a staff room or a medical room. Ensure all teachers understand the child can always go to this room without having to explain why.

Look for changes in performance and behaviour

Bereaved children may lose interest in their work, or become disruptive or withdrawn at any time. This could happen months or even years after a bereavement, but still be connected to the bereavement. If their performance or behaviour is out of character, consider that it may be due to the bereavement. Grief takes a long time and it is your job to be supportive, not demanding.

Talk regularly to the child's parent or carer - some children act OK at school but are very upset or disruptive at home, or vice-versa.

Inform the child's carer or parent if you notice any change in a bereaved child, so the carer or parent has an opportunity to talk to the child and to help them progress through their grief with continued love and support. It may be that the child has questions that have not been answered, or has particular concerns. Through conversation, you or their carer or parent may be able to resolve an issue for the child and enable that child to move forward more positively.

Case study:

Daniel knew his dad had been killed in a collision between his car and a tanker. He suddenly got very upset a year later. Through conversation, it emerged that it had struck Daniel that the tanker must have been very big, and that his dad must have been very slowly crushed to death when the tanker fell on top of his car, and his dad must have been very frightened before he died. In truth, his dad had died quickly on impact, and the tanker hadn't toppled slowly on top of the car. Daniel had never been told this. Once he knew this, he felt a bit better.